CAPE POETRY PAPERBACKS

ADRIAN HENRI
CITY HEDGES

Adrian Henri

CITY HEDGES
POEMS 1970-76

JONATHAN CAPE
THIRTY BEDFORD SQUARE LONDON

First published 1977
© 1973, 1974, 1975, 1976, 1977 by Adrian Henri

Jonathan Cape Ltd
30 Bedford Square, London WC1

British Cataloguing in Publication Data
Henri, Adrian
City hedges.
I. Title
821'.9'14   PR6058.E53C/
ISBN 0-224-01423-4

'Galactic Lovepoem Two' was first published in *Beyond This Horizon*, Ceolfrith
Press, 1973: 'The Triumph of Death', 'Lullaby' ('Woken and then lulled by the
seagulls') and 'Epilogue' in *Penguin Modern Poets Number 10, The Mersey Sound*,
1974; 'Metropolis' in *New Departures* magazine, 1975; 'Morning Song' was
first printed by Steam Press, 1975, and 'One Year' by Arc Press, 1976.

Printed in Great Britain by The Anchor Press Ltd
and bound by Wm Brendon & Son Ltd
both of Tiptree, Essex

Contents

Citysongs

Morning Song

Of meat and flowers I sing
Butchers and gardeners:

When aware of the body's process
The long journey into red night
The unfamiliar pounding that may cease at any moment
Drift off into the night full of sounds
Ticklings and murmurs, whispers and gurglings

When my mouth
Open against the open world of you
Into the darkness of rosepetals
Continents against white continents
Shudder in perspective

When the curtains are drawn
And you blossom into morning
Eyes unveiled from sleep flower-beds thrown back
White lilies against your hair's vine-leaves
I will rise and moisten the warm wet soil
to perfection:

Of meat and flowers I sing
Butchers and gardeners:
Songs thrown bleeding onto counters
Reaching up to the sun through city backyards.

Wartime

1 Hostage
in memoriam Ulrike Meinhof

Urban Guerilla
you burst into me
machinegunned
the old poems
stationed at the door
for just such a contingency
made off
with my heart
in the getaway car
despite
a desperate chase
by police in armoured cars
held it to ransom
demanding
nothing less than total involvement.

That night
a bloodless revolution
statues of the old regime
toppled in the streets
victory-fires
lit on every hillside.

Now,
in the final shootout
you fight on alone
at the window of the blazing house
I a voluntary hostage
bewildered

listen to the howl
of approaching squad-cars
taste
the stench of gas-grenades
as the masked militiamen
burst
into the room
wonder
if I'll miss you.

2 Regime

Torn posters flap
wind howls through
rusting hustings
no fate is known
for those deposed
brave new politicians
govern the bedroom
undisturbed by the sound
of distant firing-squads.

3 Truce

After the bitter end of war
and tired troops return
wounded sunbathe
hospital-blue on balconies
retreat
my undefeated lover

starshells will wake us
mysterious armies
regroup by night
between our separate bodies

tomorrow
the dawn attack
the blood-filled trenches
worlds locked again
in loving combat.

The Dance of Death

autumn to winter:
willowherb turns indigo
against the orange of its going
bonfires in backyards
hold the fitful dusk at bay
flushed childrens' faces
candles in pumpkins
strains of the 'Dies Irae' heard in the distance.

Dancing figures against the fading skyline
bony feet through withered leaves
leaping singing flapping like stormclouds
Death the Magician
conjuring darkness out of daylight
Death and the Lovers
crouching behind the settee peering through the curtains
Death and the Maiden
cold phalanxes of fingers over goosepimpled flesh
probing the warm and secret places
' ... there will now follow a party political broadcast
on behalf of Death ... this programme will be shown
on all channels ... '
Death the Politician
polished white face carefully sipping water
adjusting his fireside manner
DEATH RULES OK
scrawled on a wall outside the football stadium
Death the Terrorist Death the Avenger
O there is no hiding from the secret bomber
the parcel left unnoticed in the crowded discotheque

Death the Trafficwarden **Death** the Controller
bodies spilling everywhere
trainsmash or planecrash
carbrakes on tarmac
Death and the Soldier
familiar companion
riding a troop-carrier in camouflage gravecloths
Death and the Boatman
steering the October ferry to Eridanus
Death the Popsinger –
obscene spangled bony limbs gyrating –
Death and the Drunkard
grinning behind the barmaid's smile
Death and the Junkie
kindly refilling the hypodermic
Death and the Priest
mocking laughter from behind the altar
sly white face behind the confessional
Death and the Schoolgirl
cold hand up her gymslip in the autumn park
Death and the Farmer
following the furrow seed falling barren
Death in the Supermarket,
Corner-shop, Greengrocers',
Dance-hall and Waiting-room,
Alehouse and News-stand,
Housewife and Bunnygirl
join in the sarabande
hold hands and dance, dance
as the lightnings whirl
dance, dance, dance to the darkness ...

eve,
and the Michaelmas moon
rise in the firtrees
 ast strains of music

heard from the deadlands
November dreams
lost amongst stormclouds.

Annabel

Annabel
can't tell
home
before dark
afternoon kisses
still warm
on your lips
rain drips
from privet leaves
in city gardens

Annabel
can't say
can't stay
home before
dark
eyes
bright
through the
rainwet
streets.

For the Girl
from the Green Cabaret

for Sue Jackson

green girl
didn't grow up
don't grow up
stay like the sea
for me
every wave different
always the same
green girl

eat up the buttercups
shamed by your hair
remember what's good for you
green girl

green girl
cry rainstorms
dry your eyes with strawberry-leaves
laugh forests
at noon
sing rivers headlands islands for me
green girl

dream
girl
seen
at first light
flowers

in the night
stay
for me
green
girl.

Galactic Lovepoem Two

for *Frances*

Universes
away from you
light-years
from your sleeping back
spindrift of stars between us

after
sharing water
in the yellow desert of the bedroom
dreams
filled with insect-men
warm giants their heads made of animals
counting electric sheep
doors that talk back to you
vortices of time
torn by the alarm-clock

nebulae
in your waking eyes
time-warp
of your morning kiss
this poem for you
through the grey barricades
of daylight.

Metropolis

for David Gascoyne

I

gravelponds along long lines
fruit-trees heavy in the autumn sunlight
disturbed only by the falling brickdust
and the distant roar of engines in the morning air.

blackberries glinting in the sunlight
poised against the sky   toppling into enormous pits
hayfields   troutstreams   drystone walls
falling   tumbling   rolling before the gleaming blades
squashed hedgehogs dying owls rabbits screaming
grass and tiny bodies tangled in the clay
before the march of giant earthmovers.

O stars trees ponds
tornup roots of farmhouses
gape into the mist
allnight roar of a thousand cementmixers
acetylene lights flooding the sky.

2

apocalypsis of weirs foaming into polluted canals
endless landscape of factoryfields
chimneys belching dark into the distance
all roads home gleaming far away silver seen briefly
                            through the drifting clouds.

vast reactors megatheriums of pylons
tangled webs of cables blotting out the light
save for bright sodium-lights above the rushing expressways
flyover   cloverleaf   underpass
one way only   every which way
roadways layered up into the darkness.

3

concrete empty electric hallways
echoing with the sound of Muzak
shopfronts still boarded   shuttering still on the pillars
scaffolding everywhere through the haze
glass towers into the sky
acres of polished tables   boardroom carpet
empty halls of computers and filing cabinets.

endless escalators   vistas of plump thighs
nylon curved crammed tight with bursting flesh
tight glimpsed whitecotton secrets
soft female smell in the secret darkness
nerveless fingers immobile on trains
touching the warm imagined places
vistas of pink nipples haloed through delicate lace
disappearing out of the corners of the eyes.

NIGHT   The neon landscape
the soft purr of skysigns switching on at evening
like the roosting of longdead pigeons
nightlong litany of hammers and rockdrills
green light flickering from the wall-to-wall telescreens.

4

huge bridges   majestic arches
spanning the longdead beds of rivers
dried pramwheels   rusty cans   bones of dead animals
stagnant pools rainbowed with oil
where fishes once swarmed.

limitless vistas of bungalows and tower-flats
behind the highways
obscured constantly by the gathering darkness
ceaseless flashing of commutercars under the yellow lights
gaping mouths of endless tunnels
gleaming silver trains swish and rattle into blackness
old videotapes of trees played rushingly past the empty windows
stereo birdsong through the airconditioned silence.

Scenes from the Permissive Society

1 There were no survivors from the dawn raid ...

for Richard Hill

Soldiers of love:
returning at dawn
shock-troops
in the sex-war
dropped
2 doors away
no prisoners taken
cyanide button sewn onto lapel
excuses timed
with a self-destruct mechanism
activated
at the first sign of tears.

2 Poem to be printed on a pair of paper panties

Throw these away in the morning
Like the things we said last night
Words that go bump in the darkness
Crumpled and stained in the light

Promises made with our bodies
Dropped in the bin by the day
Look for the signs of our loving
Carefully hide them away

Straighten the folds in the bedclothes
Smooth out the pillow we shared
Tidied away in the corner
Along with our last lying words.

3
I want a love
as intimate as feminine deodorant
As easily disposed of
as paper underwear
As fresh as
the last slice of sliced bread
As instant as
flavour-rich coffee granules
As necessary as
money
Available
on demand
A love
as glossy
double-spread
full-colour
full-frontal
as a Bunny-girl
(and the only key
belongs to me)

I want a
Number One
Smooth creamy
Hi-speed
Cross-your-Heart
Getaway
Cool as a

Cosy-Glo
Fingertip control
Throwaway
Here today
Never pay
Any way
love.

Dreamsong

Astronaut
of your inner spaces
caught
in the time-warp
of your body
instruments
refusing to register
lost
in the darkness
of your star-spaces
entropy
defeated
by our loving

parallel
universes
lost
in the future

breath of starlight
on our faces
one second away
from supernova
wait
for the sound
of city morning.

Morning

Jars of you
remind
in the morning bathroom
Face Saving Lotion
face-saving motions,
face-saving motions,
crying in the late-night restaurant where we talk
                              instead of home
inviting someone back so we can't face each other
something to fill the gap after the telly stops
something to replace the tooknown records on the turntable
unsurmountable barriers of words
turn us like strangers
spaces huge as kingdoms lie between us
in the onceloved bed.

Out of the Railway Wardrobe

for Rob Conybeare

Out of the wardrobe. Out of the darkness. Out of the
railway distance. Behind the suits carefully preserved in
mothballs for the next wedding funeral divorce or
christening the seats of the trousers gleaming grey-striped or
navy-blue in the faint light from the end of the tunnel. The
tunnel whose sooty-smelling breath still holds the memory
of long-dead steam-trains. Chugging over points, the
blackened sandstone walls stretching up to the light.
Regular rows of strip-lights against the walls and clumps of
willowherb growing in crevices far above. Behind the
slightly faded wine-coloured evening dress, the wine-coloured
satin dance shoes with diamanté heels, the black afternoon
frock with the pattern of tea roses, the overhead gantries
meet the rails at the precise point of infinity. Out of the
warm musty darkness the childhood slightly scented smell
of fur-coats against your nose tickling you as you breathe in
eyes accustomed to the rustling dark the line of light round
the not-quite-closed door as the sound of metal wheels
accelerating across level-crossings grows nearer and nearer.

Out into broad daylight your unexpected city faces. Red
marsupial stranger poems clutched warm in the little pouch.

Out of the wardrobe out of the junction boxes out of the
serge and mothballs the silk and fur out of the sound of
whistles and platform-trolleys. Out of the wardrobe ...
wardrobe of dreams wardrobe of desires ... wardrobe of
upholstery smelling of tobacco-smoke ... wardrobe of the
emptiness of stations wardrobe of memories ... wardrobe of
discarded female underwear ... wardrobe of darkness ...
wardrobe where farewells hang in the glass and cast-iron

26

roof ... wardrobe of broken-down patent-leather tango-time dance-pumps ... wardrobe with hidden illicit dusty books on top wardrobe of perspectives wardrobe of forgotten encounters ... wardrobe of crashed carriages splintered sleepers the crumpled metal rusting in summer rain ... wardrobe of cheap hotel-rooms of stains on unwelcoming sheets ... wardrobe of immobility wardrobe of rushing autumn landscapes past windows ... wardrobe of old-fashioned tennis-racquets and withered rubber bathing-hats ... wardrobe where one gossamer floats in the railway carriage sunlight wardrobe where one pigeon limps along the platform ... wardrobe where dreams lie wrapped in tissuepaper like faded orange-blossom ... wardrobe where dreams wait endlessly outside Crewe Station ... wardrobe where dreams lie trapped between frozen points wardrobe where dreams hang crumpled their buttons missing ... out into daylight where dreams float away on the wind tinged with petrol fumes ... out into bright afternoon red marsupial stranger lost in a wilderness of concrete flyovers.

Citysong

angel
dark angel
constant as seasons
infrequent as words
old rainbow midnight
remembered at dawn
breath of wings
on the morning pillow
waking
with dreams in your eyes
fragments of lost conversations
on your lips

Red
Queen of my heart
locked
in the Tower
your willing victim
rivers of faces
not hearing my cries

barges
tug at the tides
helpless I drown
warehouse and Ionic column
down
before my eyes

fireweed
on demolition sites
butterfly
beneath the breaker's hammer
sing for me

Red
Queen
of my heart
mistress of my city
lady of the river

you give me

rainbows
riversides
mountains

I give you

fragments of broken dreams
bustickets
torn snapshots

You send me
anthems
psalms
symphonies

I send you
stammered words
shared bedtime-stories
failed songs
trailing away

night into day ...

waking
with the key to the woods
black cat lost
in pink-and-white flowers

night into day
Sunday churches penetrate the sky
July fifes and drums
in the William-and-Mary streets

night into day
meeting at morning
leaving at evening

night into day
soft weeds sway
in the river's fastness

night into day
down into darkness
drowning in sunlight

lady
O lady
day into midnight

last breath
on the morning pillow

silent words

forgotten seasons

angel

dark angel

sudden wings
as the clouds
close about us.

The Triumph of Death

'Thunder in the dark at Adrian Henri's ...

I
birdsong
dropping into space between the sodium-lights
footsteps echo on the wet yellow pavement
down the hill lights of the unknown hometown
bright across the river

First faint chords drift in from the orchestra
woodwinds high in the air
light from the evening sun catching the river
dockyards at the end of the street
flicker with the first smudges of flame
sudden skull-head peering from round the street-corner
seen for a moment from the top of the street
shopping-bag in hand
white beckoning skeleton hand unnoticed behind the parked
cars

darkling sky clouding the silver water

2
Fanfare of French Horns:
cars pile relentless into each other at trafficlights
grinning skeletal policemen
ride ambulances over pedestrians
klaxon-horns blaring

MUSIC FULL UP:
strings brass tympani
hoarse screams of owls from parks
despairing wail of sirens from sinking ferryboats
roar of exploding oil-tanks
walls of flame round abandoned tankers
figures of men broken on wheels against the lurid sky

high
above
squadron upon squadron
of dark figures
wheel triumphantly
row derisively amongst the carnage
salmon leap despairingly from the boiling waters

3
images from the haunted screen:

in the deserted cinema
a trapped usherette
smashes shattering the waxen mask
grinning hideous face beneath
football-crowds melting like waxworks
faces running marble eyeballs fallen from sockets
rooftops at crazy angles
dark figure in at the bedroom window
classrooms burst into flame
a skeleton exposes his rotting pelvis
to the helpless gaze of a class of schoolgirls

4

typists   shopgirls   errandboys
scream hopelessly
run towards ornamental gardens
from the falling buildings
white mocking figures insolently riding the debris
neat gardens in St James' Cemetery
torn apart
wreathed and cellophaned flowers tumbled aside
as gravecloths burst into the light
white blinking stumbling figures
queue at the gravemouths

black crows perch on the remains of department stores
dying seagulls splattered helpless against the sky
vultures wait on the Cathedral tower
busloads of darkrobed skeleton figures
raping laughing dancing singing
a revolving door spins unheeded
the hotel lounge littered with corpses

gibbets long as vermin-poles down the middle of streets
mocking roar of music behind the explosions
thunder in the dark
light only from the burning earth
dark   dark   dark
white bony mocking faces everywhere

5

And you beside me, my morning girl of the shadows
the inscrutable nurse always at the morning bedside
white breasts sprouting naked beneath your black cloak
head thrown back swirls of rivermist in your hair
take me fold me forever in your warm darkness

suck the cold life from my willing veins
lost in a final dark embrace

black barge straining waiting at the riverbank.

Annunciation

in memoriam Dmitri Shostakovich

' ... till London be a city of palm-trees'
CHRISTOPHER SMART, *Jubilate Agno*

Yes,
the prisoners shall sing in their chains
and poets burst forth from snowy prisons
the forests will liberate the badgers
and the rusting barbwire of sandy detention-camps
flower forth with evergreen
dwarf birches reach up high as redwoods
streets shall sing where our brushes have passed
black flags unfurled on every hillside

and
   yes,
the beautiful lady with the head made of flowers
will step out of your dreams into daylight
will step out into the street over the disused barricades
will glide through prisons
will appear in mineshafts
and
yes, the last pit-ponies will see again

borstal-boys dance into daylight
entire populations
write poems by the light of blazing labour-exchanges
museums disappear under clouds of butterflies
motorways buried in hydrangeas
factories producing bargain dreams

mansions of flowers
rise
on the remains of tower-blocks

and,
    yes,
through the lanes of
Shropshire Somerset Devon Normandy
where we walked
a thousand paintings shall blossom through the hedgerows
pigs picnicking on the remains of factory-farms
giant cakes stretch away magic to infinity

trees fill the bedrooms
our loving
canopied with balsam and fernleaves
thunderclouds for curtains
our bodies
seen only by the lightnings

the taste of you
always on my lips
the smell of you
always in my morning nostrils

Christmas in January
roses blazing through the snow
summer smell of rosemary
eyes dark as remembered hedges

convent-girls all in their green uniforms
will sing anthems for the Annunciation
of Joy
and,
yes,
those feet

will build
Jerusalem
here
pavilions by Antoni Gaudí
flower in every housing estate

Police-chiefs Politicians Generals Heads of Security
wander unemployed through gutted council-chambers
double agents gleefully reveal their identities
see
the white bodies of soldiers
dancing in city parks
uniforms lying mildewed in flower beds
squirrels play on abandoned troop-carriers
animals wander everywhere
my cat making her morning devotions forever

O Yes
the fox no longer fear the huntsman
nor terrace-house the bulldozer
children safe from nightingales
seals play in the wake of ferry-boats
and schoolgirls make love on the desks of classrooms
for
the Goddess
of Love
is here
The beautiful white lady
at the side of the railway line
beckons from the edge of your dreams
Yes the flower-headed lady is here
and astronauts sing her amongst the nebulae
whales boom in chorus from the depths of the oceans
orchestras of factory-whistles
foghorns hooters
loud from the estuary

spraycans write her name
on every underpass
choirs of football-fans
chant her praises
in stadiums everywhere

and
my mother
resurrected
beautiful as a movie-queen
will tango through an endless afternoon of tearooms
diamanté heels a-glitter
my father beside her
handsome as Valentino

and
  – yes –
the beautiful pink-bodied Goddess
delicate,
pale as dog-roses,
will take off peacock-winged into the sky
into the pink and yellow and iceblue
dawn shading to purple
alive with stars
tiny crescent moon
pale above our city

Yes!
out over the grey haze of railway-sidings flecked with gold
of rushing millstreams and dawn light from factories
statues of horses still shrouded in mist
past our window
bodies warm against the cold panes
past the Cathedrals out over the river
past the airfield past the dockyards
past the windows of lovers

trembling at the lightning playing round pylons
past bedsitters and farmhouses
distant as Icarus
soaring into daylight
over icecapped mountains
green wings spread into pale orange daylight

you
die away
on the still air
a tiny patter of kettledrums
the only signal
of your going.

One Year

1973-74
Liverpool – Totleigh Barton –
Hollywood – New York City –
Much Wenlock

One Year

one year:
my lady of the butterfly-tree
bright lepidoptera halo your head
dark green fritillary, brimstone and tortoiseshell
peacock and mazarine
sing anthems for the dying winter

'home is anywhere inside you
borrowed bedrooms
shared dreams'

one year:
the smell of daffodils
fills my head
springtime to springtime
spring tide to spring tide
pounds at concrete promenades

fat white geese
in muddy farmyards
along canals
pigs in appleblossom
osiers and bitter withy
the phantom drummer through the afternoon streets
last light through bushes
and childrens' faces over bridges
birds through the aspen-leaves of your body

meeting then leaving
like a rainbow in the night

unremembered kisses
gingerbread heart crumbled in a corner
enigmas of the afternoon
creeping wisteria of suburbs

our life goodbyes
the numbered silences of stations

now the land alive with butterflies
foxgloves in hedges
speedwell in clover
thorns against your sandalled feet
glittering turquoise dragonflies
against the troutbrown river

mudflats over the seawall
and woods for phantom travellers

silvergrey
seedpods of bushes
at the water's edge

summer fading to autumn
dying fireweed
drifting smoke in afternoon hedges
gone with the daylight

'borrowed bedrooms
shared dreams'

Bougainvillaea and hibiscus
bright in the California sunshine
trees from the Palmhouses of Liverpool
in everyone's garden
cries of surfers conga-drums in the afternoon
Malibu sand soft to the horizon

smell of chaparral from canyons
along the burning highway

walking along Sunset
sidewalk warm under my feet

'Hollywood Tom
at the teenage prom
in Rodney's Discotheque

strange fruit
zapote cherimoya
witches' treasures of pumpkins in supermarkets

'five minutes to kick-off
and forty-five to salvation
The Reverend Ike tells you what it's like
on your favorite T.V. station'

poet in Disneyland:
walking round
head full of images
no poem to write
a song without a singer

light fading above the HOLLYWOOD sign
last leaves of our butterfly-tree
torn by the winter rain
frayed heads of palmtrees high above the hills
high electric sound of crickets synthesized with the night

'home is anywhere
inside you'

7th Avenue Valley of Nightmares
sirens tearing my dreams apart

can't get back downtown
for the terrible rain
heaps of straining spurting flesh
out into drenching daylight

remember remember the first of November
picking 2 red leaves in Central Park for you
familiar squirrels hopping a step ahead
loving you on Long Island
fall trees auburn all bright to autumn

back again
to familiar flooded fields
last yellow of birches

bare trees
dropped leaves around their ankles

wet feet on cobblestones
dead chrysanthemums through mist

Christmas-wreaths dying
on suburban front doors

'home is anywhere inside you
neon moonlight
dawn streets'

one year
my lady
one year to tell
words lock together move together
stay apart
inexorably as seasons

waiting at demolished stations
wind from the dead land tearing us apart
two heaps of yellowing bones
sing in the intolerable sunshine

lady
do not ask me
of dry leaves pressed between bodies
dry lips grinning from underground
sing of our one-year chrysalid love
butterfly of all seasons
bright badge pinned against the painted sky

sing
of your body white against green lawns
as the morning sky declares its splendour
pale clouds curdled with blood
light running up the motorway

sing
constellations crowning your head
blossom bursting from branches
gardens painted against the sunset
sing of our seasons
appletree and oaktree
maple and holly

one
frail
butterfly
pale
against the darkening sky
lost among branches
flickers in the darkness.

Countrysongs

Evening Song

'I will come to you when the light has gone … '

I will come to you when the light has gone
When the sea has wandered far from its shores
And the hedges are drenched in evening
I will come to you when the light is gone

I will come to you when the day has gone
When butterflies disappear in the dark
And the night is alive with tiny wings
I will come to you when the day is gone

I will come to you when the night has come
And morning-glories swell in the darkness
Birds lie wrapped in nests of silence
I will come to you when the night is come

I will love you till the day has come
Trees and fields revealed in morning
Birds awake and sing the sunrise
I will love you till the day is come.

Two Lullabys

I
Here is a poem written on the clouds for you
When white bodies dance in suburban gardens
Accompanied only by the sound of lawnmowers
Champagne pouring into empty swimming-pools
Here is a poem written on the clouds for you

Here is a poem written on the sky for you
On the very last day
When skulls and hummingbirds crowd the beaches like
                                        deckchairs
Seagulls singing their final requiem
Here is a poem written on the sky for you

Here is a poem written in the air for you
When the flood is over
And pigs are left dangling in the treetops
Valleys overturned and rivers upended
Here is a poem written in the air for you

Here is a poem written on the clouds for you
When the poets are gone and the poems forgotten
When a new earth blooms
And the dying heart pumps a song of welcome
Here is a poem written on the clouds for you.

2

Woken and then lulled by the seagulls
Sleep till the sea-fret rolls by
Turn on your pillow till morning
Back to the opening sky

Sleep though the dreams may come crowding
Like mists across the bay
Night-birds will hover above you
Cry to the echoing day

Sleep though the aeroplanes lull you
Dull through the evening skies
Sleep with the seabirds for guardians
Distances lost in their eyes

Sandpipers wade on the marshes
Curlews awake on the plain
Turn to the cobblestone sunlight
Wake to the morning again.

Two Mornings

1
The little town wakes to the morning
tower four-square to the light
pink gladioli scarlet flowers of runner-beans
pinnate raspberry-leaves
coconut from the weekend fair
desiccating in the sunlight

Pink light through opened rose-leaves
yellow privet through the cottage window
the smell of rosemary from the herb-garden
mixed with last night's smell of you
on my morning fingers.

2
in the soft dawn light
2 sandpipers on white rocks stained with seaweed
bed a riot of empty oystershells
wings white barred with dark brown:
one, red-eyed, anxious, peers at the remains of last night's
                                                                meal
the other, red beak extended,
looks towards the ocean
pink-legged belly full with seed
toward implacable horizons.

A Song for A. E. Housman

I walk the lanes of Wenlock
And dream about the night
Where every leaf is shrivelled
And every berry bright

In Wenlock Town the drink goes down
The laughter flows like wine
In Wenlock Town the leaves are brown
And you're no longer mine

Day turns to night in Wenlock
Laughter to early tears
Down by the hill I follow still
The path we walked this year

Come let it snow on Wenlock
Fall down and cover me
Happy I was in Wenlock
Happy no more I'll be.

A Song for New Year's Day

Dawn drenched into sodden day
pheasant wings whirr into morning
high stones guard the hills
villages quietest under the winter sun
circled yews by rotting iron vaults
dripping to misted afternoon
late light dies on puddles along lanes
with no turnings:
now the season turns
mistletoe stamped underfoot on the bar-room floor
the hills encircle, the valleys enfold
mist tucked between like bedclothes
Christmas-lights down village streets
guard the darkness:
now is the solstice
the shortest of days
raise high the glass against the night
light fading over the hills;
still the tall stones await a winter sacrifice
black hills dark with heather
drink up forget the ghost in the chimney-corner
rattle the lock in the door
the watching and the waiting
dance in their turning
alehouse and graveyard, watcher and walker.

Drinker and dreamer move in their courses
turn with the seasons
drink with the dancers
wait for the new year's slow expiation.

Three Landscapes

1
pledged
by the wild plum-tree
kisses
only a bite away
childhood
silence
alive with gossamers.

2
red earth
stillness
lane shuttered
high
above
the sound of ash trees.

3
Dalmatian dog
spotted
against painted grass
your hair
harvested with sunlight.

Landscape, Ulster

for Edna and Michael Longley

What
do these fields
conceal?

the sheep graze as elsewhere
first signs of spring in copses
the hills the farmhouses
all normal enough

are there boobytraps
behind every blade of grass?
exploding snowdrops?
assassins lurk in every hedgerow?

only the crows walk fatter along the verges.

Night Storm

pink and white
sudden
pale yellow light
silhouettes of trees

left behind the eyes
as the thunder
tumbles
overhead

you huddle to me
a frightened rabbit
hawkwings of light
seeking you
across the darkened plain.

le Thil, Normandy

Heptonstall Memory

a limerick

In the town of the grey granite tower
With the smell of the balsam in flower
    On that final June day
    When we both went away
You turned as the clock struck the hour.

Song for Yesterday's Girl

for Dennis Woolf

Spring.
flowering cherry trees lament for lost loves
city streets echo with forgotten promises
snowdrops burst from the graves of village maidens
drowned for love in the dark pool
badgers turn out their winter beds into the red earth.

Spring,
and alcoholics blossom in city squares
first loves sprout along polluted canals
unmeant goodbyes unanswered letters
lilies-of-the-valley in florists' shops and shaded backyards
remember you with every breath.

Spring, and bitter memories sprout like tulips
melting snow reveals buried indecisions
first rhododendrons blink into sunlight
furze, and first dust of buttercups in the meadow
last daffodils die in forgotten corners.

Spring and your face through every landscape.

Butterfly

for Carol Ann Duffy

cry
for the butterfly
in your warm hand
hard light
on the threadbare tapestry of my wings
rainbow dust
left on the loved lines
of your palm

cry
with me
helpless
pinned against
stark white
black writing

sing
of your gift
for your lover
as I fall
flicker against your feet

sing
as I die
caught between intricate syllables
your song
pierce my body
butterfly
flutters

at the foot of the page
tiny rainbow
dies for your song
in the evening sunlight.

Don't Look

Don't look in my eyes, then
look at the dragonflies
glittering   look at the river

Don't listen to my words
listen to the crickets
loud in the hayfield   listen to the water

Don't touch me
don't feel my lips   my body
feel the earth alive with sedges
trefoil valerian   feel the sunlight

My lady,
these things I bring you
don't see   only know
a landscape in your body
a river in my eyes

Epilogue

for D.H.L.

Autumn
and leaves swirl at the roadside
splatter on windscreens
summer hopes gone
fears for the dark
the long night ahead
light ebbing to the slow horizon

'Autumn,
The falling fruit,
The long journey,'

Prepare for the dark
O bring it home with you
tuck it into bed
welcome him into your hearth
into your heart
the familiar stranger at the evening fireside

Wind howls in the trees
and toads curl into beds of leaves
night moves into day
moths into velvet
hedges brown with dying willow-herb

Open your door to the dark
the evening snow drift in unheeded
light dies from the sky
gather the stranger close on the pillow

seeds lie buried
safe under hedgerows
gather him to you
O gather him to you

Take the dark stranger
Cold under blankets
Gather O Gather
Alone in the darkness.